# This book belongs to:

_______________________________

## Date:

_______________________________

Website:

Username:                                  Email:

Password:

Security Question 1:

Security Answer 1:

Security Question 2:

Security Answer 2:

Notes:

Website:

Username:                                  Email:

Password:

Security Question 1:

Security Answer 1:

Security Question 2:

Security Answer 2:

Notes:

Website:

Username:                                  Email:

Password:

Security Question 1:

Security Answer 1:

Security Question 2:

Security Answer 2:

Notes:

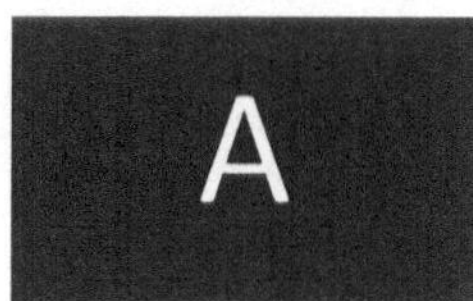


**Website:**

Username: | Email:

Password:

Security Question 1:

Security Answer 1:

Security Question 2:

Security Answer 2:

Notes:

**Website:**

Username: | Email:

Password:

Security Question 1:

Security Answer 1:

Security Question 2:

Security Answer 2:

Notes:

**Website:**

Username: | Email:

Password:

Security Question 1:

Security Answer 1:

Security Question 2:

Security Answer 2:

Notes:

**Website:**

Username: | Email:

Password:

Security Question 1:

Security Answer 1:

Security Question 2:

Security Answer 2:

Notes:

**Website:**

Username: | Email:

Password:

Security Question 1:

Security Answer 1:

Security Question 2:

Security Answer 2:

Notes:

**Website:**

Username: | Email:

Password:

Security Question 1:

Security Answer 1:

Security Question 2:

Security Answer 2:

Notes:

Website:

Username:                    Email:

Password:

Security Question 1:

Security Answer 1:

Security Question 2:

Security Answer 2:

Notes:


Website:

Username:                    Email:

Password:

Security Question 1:

Security Answer 1:

Security Question 2:

Security Answer 2:

Notes:


Website:

Username:                    Email:

Password:

Security Question 1:

Security Answer 1:

Security Question 2:

Security Answer 2:

Notes:

**Website:**

Username:      Email:

Password:

Security Question 1:

Security Answer 1:

Security Question 2:

Security Answer 2:

Notes:

---

**Website:**

Username:      Email:

Password:

Security Question 1:

Security Answer 1:

Security Question 2:

Security Answer 2:

Notes:

---

**Website:**

Username:      Email:

Password:

Security Question 1:

Security Answer 1:

Security Question 2:

Security Answer 2:

Notes:

Website:

Username:      Email:

Password:

Security Question 1:

Security Answer 1:

Security Question 2:

Security Answer 2:

Notes:

---

Website:

Username:      Email:

Password:

Security Question 1:

Security Answer 1:

Security Question 2:

Security Answer 2:

Notes:

---

Website:

Username:      Email:

Password:

Security Question 1:

Security Answer 1:

Security Question 2:

Security Answer 2:

Notes:

# B

**Website:**

Username:                              Email:

Password:

Security Question 1:

Security Answer 1:

Security Question 2:

Security Answer 2:

Notes:

**Website:**

Username:                              Email:

Password:

Security Question 1:

Security Answer 1:

Security Question 2:

Security Answer 2:

Notes:

**Website:**

Username:                              Email:

Password:

Security Question 1:

Security Answer 1:

Security Question 2:

Security Answer 2:

Notes:

**Website:**

Username:      Email:

Password:

Security Question 1:

Security Answer 1:

Security Question 2:

Security Answer 2:

Notes:

**Website:**

Username:      Email:

Password:

Security Question 1:

Security Answer 1:

Security Question 2:

Security Answer 2:

Notes:

**Website:**

Username:      Email:

Password:

Security Question 1:

Security Answer 1:

Security Question 2:

Security Answer 2:

Notes:

B

Website:

Username:      Email:

Password:

Security Question 1:

Security Answer 1:

Security Question 2:

Security Answer 2:

Notes:

---

Website:

Username:      Email:

Password:

Security Question 1:

Security Answer 1:

Security Question 2:

Security Answer 2:

Notes:

---

Website:

Username:      Email:

Password:

Security Question 1:

Security Answer 1:

Security Question 2:

Security Answer 2:

Notes:

**B**

Website:

Username:     Email:

Password:

Security Question 1:

Security Answer 1:

Security Question 2:

Security Answer 2:

Notes:


Website:

Username:     Email:

Password:

Security Question 1:

Security Answer 1:

Security Question 2:

Security Answer 2:

Notes:


Website:

Username:     Email:

Password:

Security Question 1:

Security Answer 1:

Security Question 2:

Security Answer 2:

Notes:

# B

**Website:**

Username:              Email:

Password:

Security Question 1:

Security Answer 1:

Security Question 2:

Security Answer 2:

Notes:

**Website:**

Username:              Email:

Password:

Security Question 1:

Security Answer 1:

Security Question 2:

Security Answer 2:

Notes:

**Website:**

Username:              Email:

Password:

Security Question 1:

Security Answer 1:

Security Question 2:

Security Answer 2:

Notes:

**Website:**

Username:     Email:

Password:

Security Question 1:

Security Answer 1:

Security Question 2:

Security Answer 2:

Notes:


**Website:**

Username:     Email:

Password:

Security Question 1:

Security Answer 1:

Security Question 2:

Security Answer 2:

Notes:


**Website:**

Username:     Email:

Password:

Security Question 1:

Security Answer 1:

Security Question 2:

Security Answer 2:

Notes:

# C

**Website:**

Username:        Email:

Password:

Security Question 1:

Security Answer 1:

Security Question 2:

Security Answer 2:

Notes:

---

**Website:**

Username:        Email:

Password:

Security Question 1:

Security Answer 1:

Security Question 2:

Security Answer 2:

Notes:

---

**Website:**

Username:        Email:

Password:

Security Question 1:

Security Answer 1:

Security Question 2:

Security Answer 2:

Notes:

**Website:**

Username:     Email:

Password:

Security Question 1:

Security Answer 1:

Security Question 2:

Security Answer 2:

Notes:

**Website:**

Username:     Email:

Password:

Security Question 1:

Security Answer 1:

Security Question 2:

Security Answer 2:

Notes:

**Website:**

Username:     Email:

Password:

Security Question 1:

Security Answer 1:

Security Question 2:

Security Answer 2:

Notes:

Website:

Username:      Email:

Password:

Security Question 1:

Security Answer 1:

Security Question 2:

Security Answer 2:

Notes:

Website:

Username:      Email:

Password:

Security Question 1:

Security Answer 1:

Security Question 2:

Security Answer 2:

Notes:

Website:

Username:      Email:

Password:

Security Question 1:

Security Answer 1:

Security Question 2:

Security Answer 2:

Notes:

**Website:**

Username:                          Email:

Password:

Security Question 1:

Security Answer 1:

Security Question 2:

Security Answer 2:

Notes:

**Website:**

Username:                          Email:

Password:

Security Question 1:

Security Answer 1:

Security Question 2:

Security Answer 2:

Notes:

**Website:**

Username:                          Email:

Password:

Security Question 1:

Security Answer 1:

Security Question 2:

Security Answer 2:

Notes:

**Website:**

Username:      Email:

Password:

Security Question 1:

Security Answer 1:

Security Question 2:

Security Answer 2:

Notes:

**Website:**

Username:      Email:

Password:

Security Question 1:

Security Answer 1:

Security Question 2:

Security Answer 2:

Notes:

**Website:**

Username:      Email:

Password:

Security Question 1:

Security Answer 1:

Security Question 2:

Security Answer 2:

Notes:

**Website:**

Username:                      Email:

Password:

Security Question 1:

Security Answer 1:

Security Question 2:

Security Answer 2:

Notes:


**Website:**

Username:                      Email:

Password:

Security Question 1:

Security Answer 1:

Security Question 2:

Security Answer 2:

Notes:


**Website:**

Username:                      Email:

Password:

Security Question 1:

Security Answer 1:

Security Question 2:

Security Answer 2:

Notes:

Website:

Username:                          Email:

Password:

Security Question 1:

Security Answer 1:

Security Question 2:

Security Answer 2:

Notes:


Website:

Username:                          Email:

Password:

Security Question 1:

Security Answer 1:

Security Question 2:

Security Answer 2:

Notes:


Website:

Username:                          Email:

Password:

Security Question 1:

Security Answer 1:

Security Question 2:

Security Answer 2:

Notes:

**Website:**

Username:      Email:

Password:

Security Question 1:

Security Answer 1:

Security Question 2:

Security Answer 2:

Notes:

**Website:**

Username:      Email:

Password:

Security Question 1:

Security Answer 1:

Security Question 2:

Security Answer 2:

Notes:

**Website:**

Username:      Email:

Password:

Security Question 1:

Security Answer 1:

Security Question 2:

Security Answer 2:

Notes:

Website:

Username:                    Email:

Password:

Security Question 1:

Security Answer 1:

Security Question 2:

Security Answer 2:

Notes:

Website:

Username:                    Email:

Password:

Security Question 1:

Security Answer 1:

Security Question 2:

Security Answer 2:

Notes:

Website:

Username:                    Email:

Password:

Security Question 1:

Security Answer 1:

Security Question 2:

Security Answer 2:

Notes:

D

## Website:

Username:       Email:

Password:

Security Question 1:

Security Answer 1:

Security Question 2:

Security Answer 2:

Notes:

## Website:

Username:       Email:

Password:

Security Question 1:

Security Answer 1:

Security Question 2:

Security Answer 2:

Notes:

## Website:

Username:       Email:

Password:

Security Question 1:

Security Answer 1:

Security Question 2:

Security Answer 2:

Notes:

# D



Website:

Username:                                   Email:

Password:

Security Question 1:

Security Answer 1:

Security Question 2:

Security Answer 2:

Notes:

Website:

Username:                                   Email:

Password:

Security Question 1:

Security Answer 1:

Security Question 2:

Security Answer 2:

Notes:

Website:

Username:                                   Email:

Password:

Security Question 1:

Security Answer 1:

Security Question 2:

Security Answer 2:

Notes:

Website:

Username:                          Email:

Password:

Security Question 1:

Security Answer 1:

Security Question 2:

Security Answer 2:

Notes:


Website:

Username:                          Email:

Password:

Security Question 1:

Security Answer 1:

Security Question 2:

Security Answer 2:

Notes:


Website:

Username:                          Email:

Password:

Security Question 1:

Security Answer 1:

Security Question 2:

Security Answer 2:

Notes:

**Website:**

Username: Email:

Password:

Security Question 1:

Security Answer 1:

Security Question 2:

Security Answer 2:

Notes:

**Website:**

Username: Email:

Password:

Security Question 1:

Security Answer 1:

Security Question 2:

Security Answer 2:

Notes:

**Website:**

Username: Email:

Password:

Security Question 1:

Security Answer 1:

Security Question 2:

Security Answer 2:

Notes:

**E**



Username:                    Email:

Password:

Security Question 1:

Security Answer 1:

Security Question 2:

Security Answer 2:

Notes:



Username:                    Email:

Password:

Security Question 1:

Security Answer 1:

Security Question 2:

Security Answer 2:

Notes:



Username:                    Email:

Password:

Security Question 1:

Security Answer 1:

Security Question 2:

Security Answer 2:

Notes:

Website:

Username:                                          Email:

Password:

Security Question 1:

Security Answer 1:

Security Question 2:

Security Answer 2:

Notes:


Website:

Username:                                          Email:

Password:

Security Question 1:

Security Answer 1:

Security Question 2:

Security Answer 2:

Notes:


Website:

Username:                                          Email:

Password:

Security Question 1:

Security Answer 1:

Security Question 2:

Security Answer 2:

Notes:

# E

**Website:**

Username:        Email:

Password:

Security Question 1:

Security Answer 1:

Security Question 2:

Security Answer 2:

Notes:

**Website:**

Username:        Email:

Password:

Security Question 1:

Security Answer 1:

Security Question 2:

Security Answer 2:

Notes:

**Website:**

Username:        Email:

Password:

Security Question 1:

Security Answer 1:

Security Question 2:

Security Answer 2:

Notes:

Website:

Username:                                Email:

Password:

Security Question 1:

Security Answer 1:

Security Question 2:

Security Answer 2:

Notes:


Website:

Username:                                Email:

Password:

Security Question 1:

Security Answer 1:

Security Question 2:

Security Answer 2:

Notes:


Website:

Username:                                Email:

Password:

Security Question 1:

Security Answer 1:

Security Question 2:

Security Answer 2:

Notes:

**E**

**Website:**

Username: ___________________ Email: ___________________

Password: ___________________

Security Question 1: ___________________

Security Answer 1: ___________________

Security Question 2: ___________________

Security Answer 2: ___________________

Notes: ___________________

**Website:**

Username: ___________________ Email: ___________________

Password: ___________________

Security Question 1: ___________________

Security Answer 1: ___________________

Security Question 2: ___________________

Security Answer 2: ___________________

Notes: ___________________

**Website:**

Username: ___________________ Email: ___________________

Password: ___________________

Security Question 1: ___________________

Security Answer 1: ___________________

Security Question 2: ___________________

Security Answer 2: ___________________

Notes: ___________________

**Website:**

Username:        Email:

Password:

Security Question 1:

Security Answer 1:

Security Question 2:

Security Answer 2:

Notes:

**Website:**

Username:        Email:

Password:

Security Question 1:

Security Answer 1:

Security Question 2:

Security Answer 2:

Notes:

**Website:**

Username:        Email:

Password:

Security Question 1:

Security Answer 1:

Security Question 2:

Security Answer 2:

Notes:

**F**

Website:

Username:                    Email:

Password:

Security Question 1:

Security Answer 1:

Security Question 2:

Security Answer 2:

Notes:


Website:

Username:                    Email:

Password:

Security Question 1:

Security Answer 1:

Security Question 2:

Security Answer 2:

Notes:


Website:

Username:                    Email:

Password:

Security Question 1:

Security Answer 1:

Security Question 2:

Security Answer 2:

Notes:

Website:

Username:                              Email:

Password:

Security Question 1:

Security Answer 1:

Security Question 2:

Security Answer 2:

Notes:


Website:

Username:                              Email:

Password:

Security Question 1:

Security Answer 1:

Security Question 2:

Security Answer 2:

Notes:


Website:

Username:                              Email:

Password:

Security Question 1:

Security Answer 1:

Security Question 2:

Security Answer 2:

Notes:

**F**

**Website:**

Username:                              Email:

Password:

Security Question 1:

Security Answer 1:

Security Question 2:

Security Answer 2:

Notes:

**Website:**

Username:                              Email:

Password:

Security Question 1:

Security Answer 1:

Security Question 2:

Security Answer 2:

Notes:

**Website:**

Username:                              Email:

Password:

Security Question 1:

Security Answer 1:

Security Question 2:

Security Answer 2:

Notes:

| Website: |
| --- |

| Username: | Email: |
| --- | --- |

Password:

Security Question 1:

Security Answer 1:

Security Question 2:

Security Answer 2:

Notes:

| Website: |
| --- |

| Username: | Email: |
| --- | --- |

Password:

Security Question 1:

Security Answer 1:

Security Question 2:

Security Answer 2:

Notes:

| Website: |
| --- |

| Username: | Email: |
| --- | --- |

Password:

Security Question 1:

Security Answer 1:

Security Question 2:

Security Answer 2:

Notes:

**Website:**

Username: Email:

Password:

Security Question 1:

Security Answer 1:

Security Question 2:

Security Answer 2:

Notes:

**Website:**

Username: Email:

Password:

Security Question 1:

Security Answer 1:

Security Question 2:

Security Answer 2:

Notes:

**Website:**

Username: Email:

Password:

Security Question 1:

Security Answer 1:

Security Question 2:

Security Answer 2:

Notes:

Website:

Username: | Email:

Password:

Security Question 1:

Security Answer 1:

Security Question 2:

Security Answer 2:

Notes:

Website:

Username: | Email:

Password:

Security Question 1:

Security Answer 1:

Security Question 2:

Security Answer 2:

Notes:

Website:

Username: | Email:

Password:

Security Question 1:

Security Answer 1:

Security Question 2:

Security Answer 2:

Notes:

**G**

**Website:**

Username:      Email:

Password:

Security Question 1:

Security Answer 1:

Security Question 2:

Security Answer 2:

Notes:

**Website:**

Username:      Email:

Password:

Security Question 1:

Security Answer 1:

Security Question 2:

Security Answer 2:

Notes:

**Website:**

Username:      Email:

Password:

Security Question 1:

Security Answer 1:

Security Question 2:

Security Answer 2:

Notes:

**Website:**

Username: | Email:

Password:

Security Question 1:

Security Answer 1:

Security Question 2:

Security Answer 2:

Notes:

**Website:**

Username: | Email:

Password:

Security Question 1:

Security Answer 1:

Security Question 2:

Security Answer 2:

Notes:

**Website:**

Username: | Email:

Password:

Security Question 1:

Security Answer 1:

Security Question 2:

Security Answer 2:

Notes:

# G

## Website:

Username:      Email:

Password:

Security Question 1:

Security Answer 1:

Security Question 2:

Security Answer 2:

Notes:

## Website:

Username:      Email:

Password:

Security Question 1:

Security Answer 1:

Security Question 2:

Security Answer 2:

Notes:

## Website:

Username:      Email:

Password:

Security Question 1:

Security Answer 1:

Security Question 2:

Security Answer 2:

Notes:

Website:

Username:                                        Email:

Password:

Security Question 1:

Security Answer 1:

Security Question 2:

Security Answer 2:

Notes:


Website:

Username:                                        Email:

Password:

Security Question 1:

Security Answer 1:

Security Question 2:

Security Answer 2:

Notes:


Website:

Username:                                        Email:

Password:

Security Question 1:

Security Answer 1:

Security Question 2:

Security Answer 2:

Notes:

**G**

**Website:**

Username:      Email:

Password:

Security Question 1:

Security Answer 1:

Security Question 2:

Security Answer 2:

Notes:

**Website:**

Username:      Email:

Password:

Security Question 1:

Security Answer 1:

Security Question 2:

Security Answer 2:

Notes:

**Website:**

Username:      Email:

Password:

Security Question 1:

Security Answer 1:

Security Question 2:

Security Answer 2:

Notes:

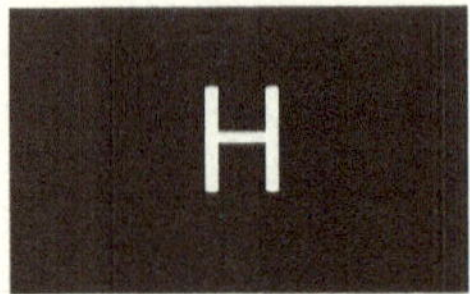

# H

---

**Website:**

Username:             Email:

Password:

Security Question 1:

Security Answer 1:

Security Question 2:

Security Answer 2:

Notes:

---

**Website:**

Username:             Email:

Password:

Security Question 1:

Security Answer 1:

Security Question 2:

Security Answer 2:

Notes:

---

**Website:**

Username:             Email:

Password:

Security Question 1:

Security Answer 1:

Security Question 2:

Security Answer 2:

Notes:

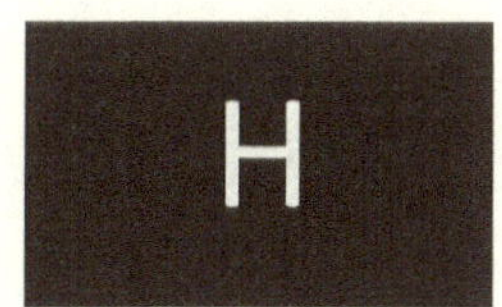



**Website:**

Username:                                    Email:

Password:

Security Question 1:

Security Answer 1:

Security Question 2:

Security Answer 2:

Notes:

---

**Website:**

Username:                                    Email:

Password:

Security Question 1:

Security Answer 1:

Security Question 2:

Security Answer 2:

Notes:

---

**Website:**

Username:                                    Email:

Password:

Security Question 1:

Security Answer 1:

Security Question 2:

Security Answer 2:

Notes:

Website:

Username:                                    Email:

Password:

Security Question 1:

Security Answer 1:

Security Question 2:

Security Answer 2:

Notes:


Website:

Username:                                    Email:

Password:

Security Question 1:

Security Answer 1:

Security Question 2:

Security Answer 2:

Notes:


Website:

Username:                                    Email:

Password:

Security Question 1:

Security Answer 1:

Security Question 2:

Security Answer 2:

Notes:

**Website:**

Username: Email:

Password:

Security Question 1:

Security Answer 1:

Security Question 2:

Security Answer 2:

Notes:

**Website:**

Username: Email:

Password:

Security Question 1:

Security Answer 1:

Security Question 2:

Security Answer 2:

Notes:

**Website:**

Username: Email:

Password:

Security Question 1:

Security Answer 1:

Security Question 2:

Security Answer 2:

Notes:

Website:

Username:                                    Email:

Password:

Security Question 1:

Security Answer 1:

Security Question 2:

Security Answer 2:

Notes:


Website:

Username:                                    Email:

Password:

Security Question 1:

Security Answer 1:

Security Question 2:

Security Answer 2:

Notes:


Website:

Username:                                    Email:

Password:

Security Question 1:

Security Answer 1:

Security Question 2:

Security Answer 2:

Notes:

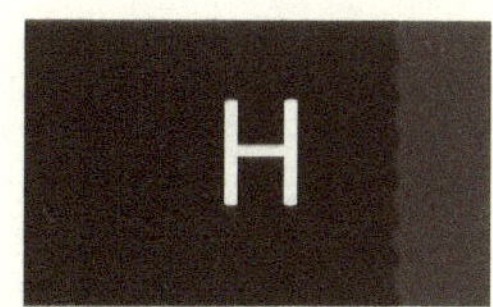


**Website:**

Username: ________________  Email: ________________

Password: ________________

Security Question 1: ________________

Security Answer 1: ________________

Security Question 2: ________________

Security Answer 2: ________________

Notes: ________________

**Website:**

Username: ________________  Email: ________________

Password: ________________

Security Question 1: ________________

Security Answer 1: ________________

Security Question 2: ________________

Security Answer 2: ________________

Notes: ________________

**Website:**

Username: ________________  Email: ________________

Password: ________________

Security Question 1: ________________

Security Answer 1: ________________

Security Question 2: ________________

Security Answer 2: ________________

Notes: ________________

Website:

Username:     Email:

Password:

Security Question 1:

Security Answer 1:

Security Question 2:

Security Answer 2:

Notes:

Website:

Username:     Email:

Password:

Security Question 1:

Security Answer 1:

Security Question 2:

Security Answer 2:

Notes:

Website:

Username:     Email:

Password:

Security Question 1:

Security Answer 1:

Security Question 2:

Security Answer 2:

Notes:

**Website:**

Username:        Email:

Password:

Security Question 1:

Security Answer 1:

Security Question 2:

Security Answer 2:

Notes:

**Website:**

Username:        Email:

Password:

Security Question 1:

Security Answer 1:

Security Question 2:

Security Answer 2:

Notes:

**Website:**

Username:        Email:

Password:

Security Question 1:

Security Answer 1:

Security Question 2:

Security Answer 2:

Notes:

| Website: |  |
| --- | --- |
| Username: | Email: |
| Password: | |
| Security Question 1: | |
| Security Answer 1: | |
| Security Question 2: | |
| Security Answer 2: | |
| Notes: | |

| Website: |  |
| --- | --- |
| Username: | Email: |
| Password: | |
| Security Question 1: | |
| Security Answer 1: | |
| Security Question 2: | |
| Security Answer 2: | |
| Notes: | |

| Website: |  |
| --- | --- |
| Username: | Email: |
| Password: | |
| Security Question 1: | |
| Security Answer 1: | |
| Security Question 2: | |
| Security Answer 2: | |
| Notes: | |

Username:                          Email:

Password:

Security Question 1:

Security Answer 1:

Security Question 2:

Security Answer 2:

Notes:


Website:

Username:                          Email:

Password:

Security Question 1:

Security Answer 1:

Security Question 2:

Security Answer 2:

Notes:


Website:

Username:                          Email:

Password:

Security Question 1:

Security Answer 1:

Security Question 2:

Security Answer 2:

Notes:

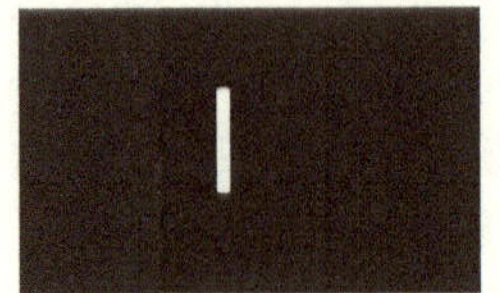

## Website:

Username:                                        Email:

Password:

Security Question 1:

Security Answer 1:

Security Question 2:

Security Answer 2:

Notes:

## Website:

Username:                                        Email:

Password:

Security Question 1:

Security Answer 1:

Security Question 2:

Security Answer 2:

Notes:

## Website:

Username:                                        Email:

Password:

Security Question 1:

Security Answer 1:

Security Question 2:

Security Answer 2:

Notes:

**Website:**

Username:        Email:

Password:

Security Question 1:

Security Answer 1:

Security Question 2:

Security Answer 2:

Notes:

**Website:**

Username:        Email:

Password:

Security Question 1:

Security Answer 1:

Security Question 2:

Security Answer 2:

Notes:

**Website:**

Username:        Email:

Password:

Security Question 1:

Security Answer 1:

Security Question 2:

Security Answer 2:

Notes:

Website:

Username:     Email:

Password:

Security Question 1:

Security Answer 1:

Security Question 2:

Security Answer 2:

Notes:

Website:

Username:     Email:

Password:

Security Question 1:

Security Answer 1:

Security Question 2:

Security Answer 2:

Notes:

Website:

Username:     Email:

Password:

Security Question 1:

Security Answer 1:

Security Question 2:

Security Answer 2:

Notes:

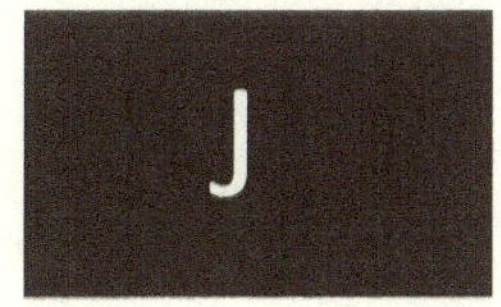


**Website:**

Username:     Email:

Password:

Security Question 1:

Security Answer 1:

Security Question 2:

Security Answer 2:

Notes:

**Website:**

Username:     Email:

Password:

Security Question 1:

Security Answer 1:

Security Question 2:

Security Answer 2:

Notes:

**Website:**

Username:     Email:

Password:

Security Question 1:

Security Answer 1:

Security Question 2:

Security Answer 2:

Notes:

**Website:**

Username: ___________________    Email: ___________________

Password: ___________________

Security Question 1: ___________________

Security Answer 1: ___________________

Security Question 2: ___________________

Security Answer 2: ___________________

Notes: ___________________

**Website:**

Username: ___________________    Email: ___________________

Password: ___________________

Security Question 1: ___________________

Security Answer 1: ___________________

Security Question 2: ___________________

Security Answer 2: ___________________

Notes: ___________________

**Website:**

Username: ___________________    Email: ___________________

Password: ___________________

Security Question 1: ___________________

Security Answer 1: ___________________

Security Question 2: ___________________

Security Answer 2: ___________________

Notes: ___________________

**Website:**

Username:      Email:

Password:

Security Question 1:

Security Answer 1:

Security Question 2:

Security Answer 2:

Notes:

**Website:**

Username:      Email:

Password:

Security Question 1:

Security Answer 1:

Security Question 2:

Security Answer 2:

Notes:

**Website:**

Username:      Email:

Password:

Security Question 1:

Security Answer 1:

Security Question 2:

Security Answer 2:

Notes:

**Website:**

Username:      Email:

Password:

Security Question 1:

Security Answer 1:

Security Question 2:

Security Answer 2:

Notes:

---

**Website:**

Username:      Email:

Password:

Security Question 1:

Security Answer 1:

Security Question 2:

Security Answer 2:

Notes:

---

**Website:**

Username:      Email:

Password:

Security Question 1:

Security Answer 1:

Security Question 2:

Security Answer 2:

Notes:

**Website:**

Username:      Email:

Password:

Security Question 1:

Security Answer 1:

Security Question 2:

Security Answer 2:

Notes:

**Website:**

Username:      Email:

Password:

Security Question 1:

Security Answer 1:

Security Question 2:

Security Answer 2:

Notes:

**Website:**

Username:      Email:

Password:

Security Question 1:

Security Answer 1:

Security Question 2:

Security Answer 2:

Notes:

---

**Website:**

Username:           Email:

Password:

Security Question 1:

Security Answer 1:

Security Question 2:

Security Answer 2:

Notes:

---

**Website:**

Username:           Email:

Password:

Security Question 1:

Security Answer 1:

Security Question 2:

Security Answer 2:

Notes:

---

**Website:**

Username:           Email:

Password:

Security Question 1:

Security Answer 1:

Security Question 2:

Security Answer 2:

Notes:

## Website:

Username:                            Email:

Password:

Security Question 1:

Security Answer 1:

Security Question 2:

Security Answer 2:

Notes:

## Website:

Username:                            Email:

Password:

Security Question 1:

Security Answer 1:

Security Question 2:

Security Answer 2:

Notes:

## Website:

Username:                            Email:

Password:

Security Question 1:

Security Answer 1:

Security Question 2:

Security Answer 2:

Notes:

Website:

Username:                                    Email:

Password:

Security Question 1:

Security Answer 1:

Security Question 2:

Security Answer 2:

Notes:


Website:

Username:                                    Email:

Password:

Security Question 1:

Security Answer 1:

Security Question 2:

Security Answer 2:

Notes:


Website:

Username:                                    Email:

Password:

Security Question 1:

Security Answer 1:

Security Question 2:

Security Answer 2:

Notes:

**Website:**

Username:      Email:

Password:

Security Question 1:

Security Answer 1:

Security Question 2:

Security Answer 2:

Notes:

**Website:**

Username:      Email:

Password:

Security Question 1:

Security Answer 1:

Security Question 2:

Security Answer 2:

Notes:

**Website:**

Username:      Email:

Password:

Security Question 1:

Security Answer 1:

Security Question 2:

Security Answer 2:

Notes:

**Website:**

Username:      Email:

Password:

Security Question 1:

Security Answer 1:

Security Question 2:

Security Answer 2:

Notes:

**Website:**

Username:      Email:

Password:

Security Question 1:

Security Answer 1:

Security Question 2:

Security Answer 2:

Notes:

**Website:**

Username:      Email:

Password:

Security Question 1:

Security Answer 1:

Security Question 2:

Security Answer 2:

Notes:

**Website:**

Username:                    Email:

Password:

Security Question 1:

Security Answer 1:

Security Question 2:

Security Answer 2:

Notes:

**Website:**

Username:                    Email:

Password:

Security Question 1:

Security Answer 1:

Security Question 2:

Security Answer 2:

Notes:

**Website:**

Username:                    Email:

Password:

Security Question 1:

Security Answer 1:

Security Question 2:

Security Answer 2:

Notes:

## Website:

Username:                               Email:

Password:

Security Question 1:

Security Answer 1:

Security Question 2:

Security Answer 2:

Notes:

## Website:

Username:                               Email:

Password:

Security Question 1:

Security Answer 1:

Security Question 2:

Security Answer 2:

Notes:

## Website:

Username:                               Email:

Password:

Security Question 1:

Security Answer 1:

Security Question 2:

Security Answer 2:

Notes:

Website:

Username:                                    Email:

Password:

Security Question 1:

Security Answer 1:

Security Question 2:

Security Answer 2:

Notes:

Website:

Username:                                    Email:

Password:

Security Question 1:

Security Answer 1:

Security Question 2:

Security Answer 2:

Notes:

Website:

Username:                                    Email:

Password:

Security Question 1:

Security Answer 1:

Security Question 2:

Security Answer 2:

Notes:

Website:

Username:                                    Email:

Password:

Security Question 1:

Security Answer 1:

Security Question 2:

Security Answer 2:

Notes:


Website:

Username:                                    Email:

Password:

Security Question 1:

Security Answer 1:

Security Question 2:

Security Answer 2:

Notes:


Website:

Username:                                    Email:

Password:

Security Question 1:

Security Answer 1:

Security Question 2:

Security Answer 2:

Notes:

# L

## Website:

Username:       Email:

Password:

Security Question 1:

Security Answer 1:

Security Question 2:

Security Answer 2:

Notes:

## Website:

Username:       Email:

Password:

Security Question 1:

Security Answer 1:

Security Question 2:

Security Answer 2:

Notes:

## Website:

Username:       Email:

Password:

Security Question 1:

Security Answer 1:

Security Question 2:

Security Answer 2:

Notes:

## L

**Website:**

Username: | Email:

Password:

Security Question 1:

Security Answer 1:

Security Question 2:

Security Answer 2:

Notes:

**Website:**

Username: | Email:

Password:

Security Question 1:

Security Answer 1:

Security Question 2:

Security Answer 2:

Notes:

**Website:**

Username: | Email:

Password:

Security Question 1:

Security Answer 1:

Security Question 2:

Security Answer 2:

Notes:

L

Website:

Username:                          Email:

Password:

Security Question 1:

Security Answer 1:

Security Question 2:

Security Answer 2:

Notes:

Website:

Username:                          Email:

Password:

Security Question 1:

Security Answer 1:

Security Question 2:

Security Answer 2:

Notes:

Website:

Username:                          Email:

Password:

Security Question 1:

Security Answer 1:

Security Question 2:

Security Answer 2:

Notes:

**Website:**

Username:            Email:

Password:

Security Question 1:

Security Answer 1:

Security Question 2:

Security Answer 2:

Notes:

**Website:**

Username:            Email:

Password:

Security Question 1:

Security Answer 1:

Security Question 2:

Security Answer 2:

Notes:

**Website:**

Username:            Email:

Password:

Security Question 1:

Security Answer 1:

Security Question 2:

Security Answer 2:

Notes:

**Website:**

Username:      Email:

Password:

Security Question 1:

Security Answer 1:

Security Question 2:

Security Answer 2:

Notes:

---

**Website:**

Username:      Email:

Password:

Security Question 1:

Security Answer 1:

Security Question 2:

Security Answer 2:

Notes:

---

**Website:**

Username:      Email:

Password:

Security Question 1:

Security Answer 1:

Security Question 2:

Security Answer 2:

Notes:

Website:

Username:                    Email:

Password:

Security Question 1:

Security Answer 1:

Security Question 2:

Security Answer 2:

Notes:


Website:

Username:                    Email:

Password:

Security Question 1:

Security Answer 1:

Security Question 2:

Security Answer 2:

Notes:


Website:

Username:                    Email:

Password:

Security Question 1:

Security Answer 1:

Security Question 2:

Security Answer 2:

Notes:

## Website:

Username:      Email:

Password:

Security Question 1:

Security Answer 1:

Security Question 2:

Security Answer 2:

Notes:

## Website:

Username:      Email:

Password:

Security Question 1:

Security Answer 1:

Security Question 2:

Security Answer 2:

Notes:

## Website:

Username:      Email:

Password:

Security Question 1:

Security Answer 1:

Security Question 2:

Security Answer 2:

Notes:

**Website:**

Username:      Email:

Password:

Security Question 1:

Security Answer 1:

Security Question 2:

Security Answer 2:

Notes:

---

**Website:**

Username:      Email:

Password:

Security Question 1:

Security Answer 1:

Security Question 2:

Security Answer 2:

Notes:

---

**Website:**

Username:      Email:

Password:

Security Question 1:

Security Answer 1:

Security Question 2:

Security Answer 2:

Notes:

**Website:**

Username: ___________________ Email: ___________________

Password: ___________________

Security Question 1: ___________________

Security Answer 1: ___________________

Security Question 2: ___________________

Security Answer 2: ___________________

Notes: ___________________

**Website:**

Username: ___________________ Email: ___________________

Password: ___________________

Security Question 1: ___________________

Security Answer 1: ___________________

Security Question 2: ___________________

Security Answer 2: ___________________

Notes: ___________________

**Website:**

Username: ___________________ Email: ___________________

Password: ___________________

Security Question 1: ___________________

Security Answer 1: ___________________

Security Question 2: ___________________

Security Answer 2: ___________________

Notes: ___________________

## Website:

Username:        Email:

Password:

Security Question 1:

Security Answer 1:

Security Question 2:

Security Answer 2:

Notes:

## Website:

Username:        Email:

Password:

Security Question 1:

Security Answer 1:

Security Question 2:

Security Answer 2:

Notes:

## Website:

Username:        Email:

Password:

Security Question 1:

Security Answer 1:

Security Question 2:

Security Answer 2:

Notes:

**N**

**Website:**

Username: | Email:

Password:

Security Question 1:

Security Answer 1:

Security Question 2:

Security Answer 2:

Notes:

**Website:**

Username: | Email:

Password:

Security Question 1:

Security Answer 1:

Security Question 2:

Security Answer 2:

Notes:

**Website:**

Username: | Email:

Password:

Security Question 1:

Security Answer 1:

Security Question 2:

Security Answer 2:

Notes:

| Website: | |
| --- | --- |
| Username: | Email: |
| Password: | |
| Security Question 1: | |
| Security Answer 1: | |
| Security Question 2: | |
| Security Answer 2: | |
| Notes: | |

| Website: | |
| --- | --- |
| Username: | Email: |
| Password: | |
| Security Question 1: | |
| Security Answer 1: | |
| Security Question 2: | |
| Security Answer 2: | |
| Notes: | |

| Website: | |
| --- | --- |
| Username: | Email: |
| Password: | |
| Security Question 1: | |
| Security Answer 1: | |
| Security Question 2: | |
| Security Answer 2: | |
| Notes: | |

N

Website:

Username:            Email:

Password:

Security Question 1:

Security Answer 1:

Security Question 2:

Security Answer 2:

Notes:

Website:

Username:            Email:

Password:

Security Question 1:

Security Answer 1:

Security Question 2:

Security Answer 2:

Notes:

Website:

Username:            Email:

Password:

Security Question 1:

Security Answer 1:

Security Question 2:

Security Answer 2:

Notes:

**Website:**

Username:        Email:

Password:

Security Question 1:

Security Answer 1:

Security Question 2:

Security Answer 2:

Notes:

---

**Website:**

Username:        Email:

Password:

Security Question 1:

Security Answer 1:

Security Question 2:

Security Answer 2:

Notes:

---

**Website:**

Username:        Email:

Password:

Security Question 1:

Security Answer 1:

Security Question 2:

Security Answer 2:

Notes:

N

**Website:**

Username:      Email:

Password:

Security Question 1:

Security Answer 1:

Security Question 2:

Security Answer 2:

Notes:

**Website:**

Username:      Email:

Password:

Security Question 1:

Security Answer 1:

Security Question 2:

Security Answer 2:

Notes:

**Website:**

Username:      Email:

Password:

Security Question 1:

Security Answer 1:

Security Question 2:

Security Answer 2:

Notes:

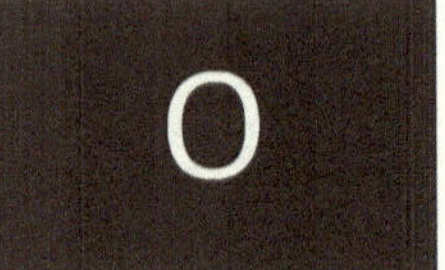



Website:

Username:                                      Email:

Password:

Security Question 1:

Security Answer 1:

Security Question 2:

Security Answer 2:

Notes:

Website:

Username:                                      Email:

Password:

Security Question 1:

Security Answer 1:

Security Question 2:

Security Answer 2:

Notes:

Website:

Username:                                      Email:

Password:

Security Question 1:

Security Answer 1:

Security Question 2:

Security Answer 2:

Notes:

**Website:**

Username:                   Email:

Password:

Security Question 1:

Security Answer 1:

Security Question 2:

Security Answer 2:

Notes:

**Website:**

Username:                   Email:

Password:

Security Question 1:

Security Answer 1:

Security Question 2:

Security Answer 2:

Notes:

**Website:**

Username:                   Email:

Password:

Security Question 1:

Security Answer 1:

Security Question 2:

Security Answer 2:

Notes:

Website:

Username: Email:

Password:

Security Question 1:

Security Answer 1:

Security Question 2:

Security Answer 2:

Notes:

---

Website:

Username: Email:

Password:

Security Question 1:

Security Answer 1:

Security Question 2:

Security Answer 2:

Notes:

---

Website:

Username: Email:

Password:

Security Question 1:

Security Answer 1:

Security Question 2:

Security Answer 2:

Notes:

# O

Website:

Username:                    Email:

Password:

Security Question 1:

Security Answer 1:

Security Question 2:

Security Answer 2:

Notes:


Website:

Username:                    Email:

Password:

Security Question 1:

Security Answer 1:

Security Question 2:

Security Answer 2:

Notes:


Website:

Username:                    Email:

Password:

Security Question 1:

Security Answer 1:

Security Question 2:

Security Answer 2:

Notes:

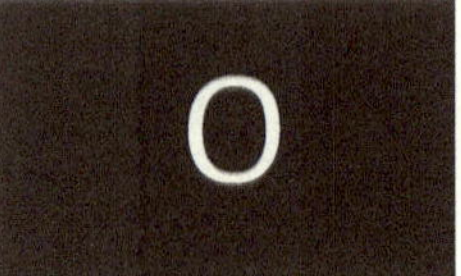


**Website:**

Username:                     Email:

Password:

Security Question 1:

Security Answer 1:

Security Question 2:

Security Answer 2:

Notes:

**Website:**

Username:                     Email:

Password:

Security Question 1:

Security Answer 1:

Security Question 2:

Security Answer 2:

Notes:

**Website:**

Username:                     Email:

Password:

Security Question 1:

Security Answer 1:

Security Question 2:

Security Answer 2:

Notes:

Website:

Username: _______________ Email: _______________

Password: _______________

Security Question 1: _______________

Security Answer 1: _______________

Security Question 2: _______________

Security Answer 2: _______________

Notes: _______________

Website:

Username: _______________ Email: _______________

Password: _______________

Security Question 1: _______________

Security Answer 1: _______________

Security Question 2: _______________

Security Answer 2: _______________

Notes: _______________

Website:

Username: _______________ Email: _______________

Password: _______________

Security Question 1: _______________

Security Answer 1: _______________

Security Question 2: _______________

Security Answer 2: _______________

Notes: _______________

**Website:**

Username:                                    Email:

Password:

Security Question 1:

Security Answer 1:

Security Question 2:

Security Answer 2:

Notes:

**Website:**

Username:                                    Email:

Password:

Security Question 1:

Security Answer 1:

Security Question 2:

Security Answer 2:

Notes:

**Website:**

Username:                                    Email:

Password:

Security Question 1:

Security Answer 1:

Security Question 2:

Security Answer 2:

Notes:

# P

**Website:**

Username:                    Email:

Password:

Security Question 1:

Security Answer 1:

Security Question 2:

Security Answer 2:

Notes:

**Website:**

Username:                    Email:

Password:

Security Question 1:

Security Answer 1:

Security Question 2:

Security Answer 2:

Notes:

**Website:**

Username:                    Email:

Password:

Security Question 1:

Security Answer 1:

Security Question 2:

Security Answer 2:

Notes:

**P**

---

**Website:**

Username:        Email:

Password:

Security Question 1:

Security Answer 1:

Security Question 2:

Security Answer 2:

Notes:

---

**Website:**

Username:        Email:

Password:

Security Question 1:

Security Answer 1:

Security Question 2:

Security Answer 2:

Notes:

---

**Website:**

Username:        Email:

Password:

Security Question 1:

Security Answer 1:

Security Question 2:

Security Answer 2:

Notes:

P

Website:

Username:                          Email:

Password:

Security Question 1:

Security Answer 1:

Security Question 2:

Security Answer 2:

Notes:


Website:

Username:                          Email:

Password:

Security Question 1:

Security Answer 1:

Security Question 2:

Security Answer 2:

Notes:


Website:

Username:                          Email:

Password:

Security Question 1:

Security Answer 1:

Security Question 2:

Security Answer 2:

Notes:

## Website:

Username: | Email:

Password:

Security Question 1:

Security Answer 1:

Security Question 2:

Security Answer 2:

Notes:

## Website:

Username: | Email:

Password:

Security Question 1:

Security Answer 1:

Security Question 2:

Security Answer 2:

Notes:

## Website:

Username: | Email:

Password:

Security Question 1:

Security Answer 1:

Security Question 2:

Security Answer 2:

Notes:

**Website:**

Username:                                    Email:

Password:

Security Question 1:

Security Answer 1:

Security Question 2:

Security Answer 2:

Notes:


**Website:**

Username:                                    Email:

Password:

Security Question 1:

Security Answer 1:

Security Question 2:

Security Answer 2:

Notes:


**Website:**

Username:                                    Email:

Password:

Security Question 1:

Security Answer 1:

Security Question 2:

Security Answer 2:

Notes:

## Website:

Username:            Email:

Password:

Security Question 1:

Security Answer 1:

Security Question 2:

Security Answer 2:

Notes:

## Website:

Username:            Email:

Password:

Security Question 1:

Security Answer 1:

Security Question 2:

Security Answer 2:

Notes:

## Website:

Username:            Email:

Password:

Security Question 1:

Security Answer 1:

Security Question 2:

Security Answer 2:

Notes:

Website:

Username:                     Email:

Password:

Security Question 1:

Security Answer 1:

Security Question 2:

Security Answer 2:

Notes:

---

Website:

Username:                     Email:

Password:

Security Question 1:

Security Answer 1:

Security Question 2:

Security Answer 2:

Notes:

---

Website:

Username:                     Email:

Password:

Security Question 1:

Security Answer 1:

Security Question 2:

Security Answer 2:

Notes:

| Website: |
| --- |

| Username: | Email: |
| --- | --- |

Password:

Security Question 1:

Security Answer 1:

Security Question 2:

Security Answer 2:

Notes:

| Website: |
| --- |

| Username: | Email: |
| --- | --- |

Password:

Security Question 1:

Security Answer 1:

Security Question 2:

Security Answer 2:

Notes:

| Website: |
| --- |

| Username: | Email: |
| --- | --- |

Password:

Security Question 1:

Security Answer 1:

Security Question 2:

Security Answer 2:

Notes:

**Website:**

Username: ___________________  Email: ___________________

Password: ___________________

Security Question 1: ___________________

Security Answer 1: ___________________

Security Question 2: ___________________

Security Answer 2: ___________________

Notes: ___________________

**Website:**

Username: ___________________  Email: ___________________

Password: ___________________

Security Question 1: ___________________

Security Answer 1: ___________________

Security Question 2: ___________________

Security Answer 2: ___________________

Notes: ___________________

**Website:**

Username: ___________________  Email: ___________________

Password: ___________________

Security Question 1: ___________________

Security Answer 1: ___________________

Security Question 2: ___________________

Security Answer 2: ___________________

Notes: ___________________

Website:

Username:     Email:

Password:

Security Question 1:

Security Answer 1:

Security Question 2:

Security Answer 2:

Notes:

---

Website:

Username:     Email:

Password:

Security Question 1:

Security Answer 1:

Security Question 2:

Security Answer 2:

Notes:

---

Website:

Username:     Email:

Password:

Security Question 1:

Security Answer 1:

Security Question 2:

Security Answer 2:

Notes:

Website:

Username:                    Email:

Password:

Security Question 1:

Security Answer 1:

Security Question 2:

Security Answer 2:

Notes:

Website:

Username:                    Email:

Password:

Security Question 1:

Security Answer 1:

Security Question 2:

Security Answer 2:

Notes:

Website:

Username:                    Email:

Password:

Security Question 1:

Security Answer 1:

Security Question 2:

Security Answer 2:

Notes:

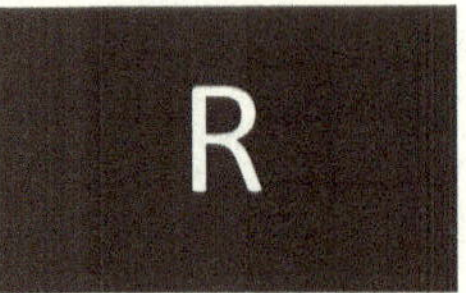

| Website: |
| --- |

| Username: | Email: |
| --- | --- |

Password:

Security Question 1:

Security Answer 1:

Security Question 2:

Security Answer 2:

Notes:

| Website: |
| --- |

| Username: | Email: |
| --- | --- |

Password:

Security Question 1:

Security Answer 1:

Security Question 2:

Security Answer 2:

Notes:

| Website: |
| --- |

| Username: | Email: |
| --- | --- |

Password:

Security Question 1:

Security Answer 1:

Security Question 2:

Security Answer 2:

Notes:

Website:

Username:                                    Email:

Password:

Security Question 1:

Security Answer 1:

Security Question 2:

Security Answer 2:

Notes:


Website:

Username:                                    Email:

Password:

Security Question 1:

Security Answer 1:

Security Question 2:

Security Answer 2:

Notes:


Website:

Username:                                    Email:

Password:

Security Question 1:

Security Answer 1:

Security Question 2:

Security Answer 2:

Notes:

Website:

Username:                                    Email:

Password:

Security Question 1:

Security Answer 1:

Security Question 2:

Security Answer 2:

Notes:


Website:

Username:                                    Email:

Password:

Security Question 1:

Security Answer 1:

Security Question 2:

Security Answer 2:

Notes:


Website:

Username:                                    Email:

Password:

Security Question 1:

Security Answer 1:

Security Question 2:

Security Answer 2:

Notes:

R

**Website:**

Username: ___________________  Email: ___________________

Password: ___________________

Security Question 1: ___________________

Security Answer 1: ___________________

Security Question 2: ___________________

Security Answer 2: ___________________

Notes: ___________________

**Website:**

Username: ___________________  Email: ___________________

Password: ___________________

Security Question 1: ___________________

Security Answer 1: ___________________

Security Question 2: ___________________

Security Answer 2: ___________________

Notes: ___________________

**Website:**

Username: ___________________  Email: ___________________

Password: ___________________

Security Question 1: ___________________

Security Answer 1: ___________________

Security Question 2: ___________________

Security Answer 2: ___________________

Notes: ___________________

**Website:**

Username:                                    Email:

Password:

Security Question 1:

Security Answer 1:

Security Question 2:

Security Answer 2:

Notes:

**Website:**

Username:                                    Email:

Password:

Security Question 1:

Security Answer 1:

Security Question 2:

Security Answer 2:

Notes:

**Website:**

Username:                                    Email:

Password:

Security Question 1:

Security Answer 1:

Security Question 2:

Security Answer 2:

Notes:

Website:

Username:                                  Email:

Password:

Security Question 1:

Security Answer 1:

Security Question 2:

Security Answer 2:

Notes:


Website:

Username:                                  Email:

Password:

Security Question 1:

Security Answer 1:

Security Question 2:

Security Answer 2:

Notes:


Website:

Username:                                  Email:

Password:

Security Question 1:

Security Answer 1:

Security Question 2:

Security Answer 2:

Notes:

# S

**Website:**

Username: ___________________  Email: ___________________

Password: ___________________

Security Question 1: ___________________

Security Answer 1: ___________________

Security Question 2: ___________________

Security Answer 2: ___________________

Notes: ___________________

**Website:**

Username: ___________________  Email: ___________________

Password: ___________________

Security Question 1: ___________________

Security Answer 1: ___________________

Security Question 2: ___________________

Security Answer 2: ___________________

Notes: ___________________

**Website:**

Username: ___________________  Email: ___________________

Password: ___________________

Security Question 1: ___________________

Security Answer 1: ___________________

Security Question 2: ___________________

Security Answer 2: ___________________

Notes: ___________________

## S

**Website:**

Username: Email:

Password:

Security Question 1:

Security Answer 1:

Security Question 2:

Security Answer 2:

Notes:

**Website:**

Username: Email:

Password:

Security Question 1:

Security Answer 1:

Security Question 2:

Security Answer 2:

Notes:

**Website:**

Username: Email:

Password:

Security Question 1:

Security Answer 1:

Security Question 2:

Security Answer 2:

Notes:

## Website:

Username:                     Email:

Password:

Security Question 1:

Security Answer 1:

Security Question 2:

Security Answer 2:

Notes:

## Website:

Username:                     Email:

Password:

Security Question 1:

Security Answer 1:

Security Question 2:

Security Answer 2:

Notes:

## Website:

Username:                     Email:

Password:

Security Question 1:

Security Answer 1:

Security Question 2:

Security Answer 2:

Notes:

# S

**Website:**

Username:                    Email:

Password:

Security Question 1:

Security Answer 1:

Security Question 2:

Security Answer 2:

Notes:

**Website:**

Username:                    Email:

Password:

Security Question 1:

Security Answer 1:

Security Question 2:

Security Answer 2:

Notes:

**Website:**

Username:                    Email:

Password:

Security Question 1:

Security Answer 1:

Security Question 2:

Security Answer 2:

Notes:

# S

**Website:**

Username:           Email:

Password:

Security Question 1:

Security Answer 1:

Security Question 2:

Security Answer 2:

Notes:

**Website:**

Username:           Email:

Password:

Security Question 1:

Security Answer 1:

Security Question 2:

Security Answer 2:

Notes:

**Website:**

Username:           Email:

Password:

Security Question 1:

Security Answer 1:

Security Question 2:

Security Answer 2:

Notes:

**S**

**Website:**

Username:            Email:

Password:

Security Question 1:

Security Answer 1:

Security Question 2:

Security Answer 2:

Notes:

**Website:**

Username:            Email:

Password:

Security Question 1:

Security Answer 1:

Security Question 2:

Security Answer 2:

Notes:

**Website:**

Username:            Email:

Password:

Security Question 1:

Security Answer 1:

Security Question 2:

Security Answer 2:

Notes:

**Website:**

Username: ___________________  Email: ___________________

Password: ___________________

Security Question 1: ___________________

Security Answer 1: ___________________

Security Question 2: ___________________

Security Answer 2: ___________________

Notes: ___________________

**Website:**

Username: ___________________  Email: ___________________

Password: ___________________

Security Question 1: ___________________

Security Answer 1: ___________________

Security Question 2: ___________________

Security Answer 2: ___________________

Notes: ___________________

**Website:**

Username: ___________________  Email: ___________________

Password: ___________________

Security Question 1: ___________________

Security Answer 1: ___________________

Security Question 2: ___________________

Security Answer 2: ___________________

Notes: ___________________

**T**

## Website:

Username: ___________________ Email: ___________________

Password: ___________________

Security Question 1: ___________________

Security Answer 1: ___________________

Security Question 2: ___________________

Security Answer 2: ___________________

Notes: ___________________

## Website:

Username: ___________________ Email: ___________________

Password: ___________________

Security Question 1: ___________________

Security Answer 1: ___________________

Security Question 2: ___________________

Security Answer 2: ___________________

Notes: ___________________

## Website:

Username: ___________________ Email: ___________________

Password: ___________________

Security Question 1: ___________________

Security Answer 1: ___________________

Security Question 2: ___________________

Security Answer 2: ___________________

Notes: ___________________

Website:

Username:                                    Email:

Password:

Security Question 1:

Security Answer 1:

Security Question 2:

Security Answer 2:

Notes:


Website:

Username:                                    Email:

Password:

Security Question 1:

Security Answer 1:

Security Question 2:

Security Answer 2:

Notes:


Website:

Username:                                    Email:

Password:

Security Question 1:

Security Answer 1:

Security Question 2:

Security Answer 2:

Notes:

**T**

Website:

Username:                    Email:

Password:

Security Question 1:

Security Answer 1:

Security Question 2:

Security Answer 2:

Notes:

---

Website:

Username:                    Email:

Password:

Security Question 1:

Security Answer 1:

Security Question 2:

Security Answer 2:

Notes:

---

Website:

Username:                    Email:

Password:

Security Question 1:

Security Answer 1:

Security Question 2:

Security Answer 2:

Notes:

**Website:**

Username:      Email:

Password:

Security Question 1:

Security Answer 1:

Security Question 2:

Security Answer 2:

Notes:

**Website:**

Username:      Email:

Password:

Security Question 1:

Security Answer 1:

Security Question 2:

Security Answer 2:

Notes:

**Website:**

Username:      Email:

Password:

Security Question 1:

Security Answer 1:

Security Question 2:

Security Answer 2:

Notes:

**Website:**

Username: | Email:

Password:

Security Question 1:

Security Answer 1:

Security Question 2:

Security Answer 2:

Notes:

**Website:**

Username: | Email:

Password:

Security Question 1:

Security Answer 1:

Security Question 2:

Security Answer 2:

Notes:

**Website:**

Username: | Email:

Password:

Security Question 1:

Security Answer 1:

Security Question 2:

Security Answer 2:

Notes:

Website:

Username:       Email:

Password:

Security Question 1:

Security Answer 1:

Security Question 2:

Security Answer 2:

Notes:


Website:

Username:       Email:

Password:

Security Question 1:

Security Answer 1:

Security Question 2:

Security Answer 2:

Notes:


Website:

Username:       Email:

Password:

Security Question 1:

Security Answer 1:

Security Question 2:

Security Answer 2:

Notes:

## Website:

Username:                 Email:

Password:

Security Question 1:

Security Answer 1:

Security Question 2:

Security Answer 2:

Notes:

## Website:

Username:                 Email:

Password:

Security Question 1:

Security Answer 1:

Security Question 2:

Security Answer 2:

Notes:

## Website:

Username:                 Email:

Password:

Security Question 1:

Security Answer 1:

Security Question 2:

Security Answer 2:

Notes:

## Website:

Username:                                   Email:

Password:

Security Question 1:

Security Answer 1:

Security Question 2:

Security Answer 2:

Notes:

## Website:

Username:                                   Email:

Password:

Security Question 1:

Security Answer 1:

Security Question 2:

Security Answer 2:

Notes:

## Website:

Username:                                   Email:

Password:

Security Question 1:

Security Answer 1:

Security Question 2:

Security Answer 2:

Notes:

**Website:**

Username:       Email:

Password:

Security Question 1:

Security Answer 1:

Security Question 2:

Security Answer 2:

Notes:

**Website:**

Username:       Email:

Password:

Security Question 1:

Security Answer 1:

Security Question 2:

Security Answer 2:

Notes:

**Website:**

Username:       Email:

Password:

Security Question 1:

Security Answer 1:

Security Question 2:

Security Answer 2:

Notes:

Website:

Username:      Email:

Password:

Security Question 1:

Security Answer 1:

Security Question 2:

Security Answer 2:

Notes:

Website:

Username:      Email:

Password:

Security Question 1:

Security Answer 1:

Security Question 2:

Security Answer 2:

Notes:

Website:

Username:      Email:

Password:

Security Question 1:

Security Answer 1:

Security Question 2:

Security Answer 2:

Notes:

## U

**Website:**

Username:                          Email:

Password:

Security Question 1:

Security Answer 1:

Security Question 2:

Security Answer 2:

Notes:


**Website:**

Username:                          Email:

Password:

Security Question 1:

Security Answer 1:

Security Question 2:

Security Answer 2:

Notes:


**Website:**

Username:                          Email:

Password:

Security Question 1:

Security Answer 1:

Security Question 2:

Security Answer 2:

Notes:

<table>
<tr><td colspan="2">Website:</td></tr>
<tr><td>Username:</td><td>Email:</td></tr>
<tr><td colspan="2">Password:</td></tr>
<tr><td colspan="2">Security Question 1:</td></tr>
<tr><td colspan="2">Security Answer 1:</td></tr>
<tr><td colspan="2">Security Question 2:</td></tr>
<tr><td colspan="2">Security Answer 2:</td></tr>
<tr><td colspan="2">Notes:</td></tr>
</table>

<table>
<tr><td colspan="2">Website:</td></tr>
<tr><td>Username:</td><td>Email:</td></tr>
<tr><td colspan="2">Password:</td></tr>
<tr><td colspan="2">Security Question 1:</td></tr>
<tr><td colspan="2">Security Answer 1:</td></tr>
<tr><td colspan="2">Security Question 2:</td></tr>
<tr><td colspan="2">Security Answer 2:</td></tr>
<tr><td colspan="2">Notes:</td></tr>
</table>

<table>
<tr><td colspan="2">Website:</td></tr>
<tr><td>Username:</td><td>Email:</td></tr>
<tr><td colspan="2">Password:</td></tr>
<tr><td colspan="2">Security Question 1:</td></tr>
<tr><td colspan="2">Security Answer 1:</td></tr>
<tr><td colspan="2">Security Question 2:</td></tr>
<tr><td colspan="2">Security Answer 2:</td></tr>
<tr><td colspan="2">Notes:</td></tr>
</table>

Website:

Username:                                    Email:

Password:

Security Question 1:

Security Answer 1:

Security Question 2:

Security Answer 2:

Notes:


Website:

Username:                                    Email:

Password:

Security Question 1:

Security Answer 1:

Security Question 2:

Security Answer 2:

Notes:


Website:

Username:                                    Email:

Password:

Security Question 1:

Security Answer 1:

Security Question 2:

Security Answer 2:

Notes:

Website:

Username:                                    Email:

Password:

Security Question 1:

Security Answer 1:

Security Question 2:

Security Answer 2:

Notes:


Website:

Username:                                    Email:

Password:

Security Question 1:

Security Answer 1:

Security Question 2:

Security Answer 2:

Notes:


Website:

Username:                                    Email:

Password:

Security Question 1:

Security Answer 1:

Security Question 2:

Security Answer 2:

Notes:

## Website:

Username: ___________________ Email: ___________________

Password: ___________________

Security Question 1: ___________________

Security Answer 1: ___________________

Security Question 2: ___________________

Security Answer 2: ___________________

Notes: ___________________

## Website:

Username: ___________________ Email: ___________________

Password: ___________________

Security Question 1: ___________________

Security Answer 1: ___________________

Security Question 2: ___________________

Security Answer 2: ___________________

Notes: ___________________

## Website:

Username: ___________________ Email: ___________________

Password: ___________________

Security Question 1: ___________________

Security Answer 1: ___________________

Security Question 2: ___________________

Security Answer 2: ___________________

Notes: ___________________

Website:

Username:                                          Email:

Password:

Security Question 1:

Security Answer 1:

Security Question 2:

Security Answer 2:

Notes:


Website:

Username:                                          Email:

Password:

Security Question 1:

Security Answer 1:

Security Question 2:

Security Answer 2:

Notes:


Website:

Username:                                          Email:

Password:

Security Question 1:

Security Answer 1:

Security Question 2:

Security Answer 2:

Notes:

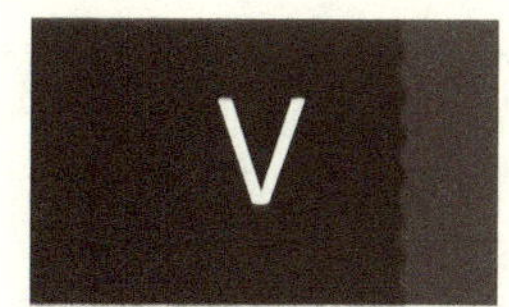

## Website:

Username:                          Email:

Password:

Security Question 1:

Security Answer 1:

Security Question 2:

Security Answer 2:

Notes:


## Website:

Username:                          Email:

Password:

Security Question 1:

Security Answer 1:

Security Question 2:

Security Answer 2:

Notes:


## Website:

Username:                          Email:

Password:

Security Question 1:

Security Answer 1:

Security Question 2:

Security Answer 2:

Notes:

Website:

Username:                                    Email:

Password:

Security Question 1:

Security Answer 1:

Security Question 2:

Security Answer 2:

Notes:

Website:

Username:                                    Email:

Password:

Security Question 1:

Security Answer 1:

Security Question 2:

Security Answer 2:

Notes:

Website:

Username:                                    Email:

Password:

Security Question 1:

Security Answer 1:

Security Question 2:

Security Answer 2:

Notes:

**Website:**

Username:            Email:

Password:

Security Question 1:

Security Answer 1:

Security Question 2:

Security Answer 2:

Notes:

**Website:**

Username:            Email:

Password:

Security Question 1:

Security Answer 1:

Security Question 2:

Security Answer 2:

Notes:

**Website:**

Username:            Email:

Password:

Security Question 1:

Security Answer 1:

Security Question 2:

Security Answer 2:

Notes:

Website:

Username:                              Email:

Password:

Security Question 1:

Security Answer 1:

Security Question 2:

Security Answer 2:

Notes:


Website:

Username:                              Email:

Password:

Security Question 1:

Security Answer 1:

Security Question 2:

Security Answer 2:

Notes:


Website:

Username:                              Email:

Password:

Security Question 1:

Security Answer 1:

Security Question 2:

Security Answer 2:

Notes:

**Website:**

Username: | Email:

Password:

Security Question 1:

Security Answer 1:

Security Question 2:

Security Answer 2:

Notes:

**Website:**

Username: | Email:

Password:

Security Question 1:

Security Answer 1:

Security Question 2:

Security Answer 2:

Notes:

**Website:**

Username: | Email:

Password:

Security Question 1:

Security Answer 1:

Security Question 2:

Security Answer 2:

Notes:

**Website:**

Username:        Email:

Password:

Security Question 1:

Security Answer 1:

Security Question 2:

Security Answer 2:

Notes:

---

**Website:**

Username:        Email:

Password:

Security Question 1:

Security Answer 1:

Security Question 2:

Security Answer 2:

Notes:

---

**Website:**

Username:        Email:

Password:

Security Question 1:

Security Answer 1:

Security Question 2:

Security Answer 2:

Notes:

**Website:**

Username:     Email:

Password:

Security Question 1:

Security Answer 1:

Security Question 2:

Security Answer 2:

Notes:

**Website:**

Username:     Email:

Password:

Security Question 1:

Security Answer 1:

Security Question 2:

Security Answer 2:

Notes:

**Website:**

Username:     Email:

Password:

Security Question 1:

Security Answer 1:

Security Question 2:

Security Answer 2:

Notes:

Website:

Username:     Email:

Password:

Security Question 1:

Security Answer 1:

Security Question 2:

Security Answer 2:

Notes:

Website:

Username:     Email:

Password:

Security Question 1:

Security Answer 1:

Security Question 2:

Security Answer 2:

Notes:

Website:

Username:     Email:

Password:

Security Question 1:

Security Answer 1:

Security Question 2:

Security Answer 2:

Notes:

**Website:**

Username:            Email:

Password:

Security Question 1:

Security Answer 1:

Security Question 2:

Security Answer 2:

Notes:

**Website:**

Username:            Email:

Password:

Security Question 1:

Security Answer 1:

Security Question 2:

Security Answer 2:

Notes:

**Website:**

Username:            Email:

Password:

Security Question 1:

Security Answer 1:

Security Question 2:

Security Answer 2:

Notes:

Website:

Username:                                        Email:

Password:

Security Question 1:

Security Answer 1:

Security Question 2:

Security Answer 2:

Notes:


Website:

Username:                                        Email:

Password:

Security Question 1:

Security Answer 1:

Security Question 2:

Security Answer 2:

Notes:


Website:

Username:                                        Email:

Password:

Security Question 1:

Security Answer 1:

Security Question 2:

Security Answer 2:

Notes:

Website:

Username:                                    Email:

Password:

Security Question 1:

Security Answer 1:

Security Question 2:

Security Answer 2:

Notes:


Website:

Username:                                    Email:

Password:

Security Question 1:

Security Answer 1:

Security Question 2:

Security Answer 2:

Notes:


Website:

Username:                                    Email:

Password:

Security Question 1:

Security Answer 1:

Security Question 2:

Security Answer 2:

Notes:

**Website:**

Username:       Email:

Password:

Security Question 1:

Security Answer 1:

Security Question 2:

Security Answer 2:

Notes:

**Website:**

Username:       Email:

Password:

Security Question 1:

Security Answer 1:

Security Question 2:

Security Answer 2:

Notes:

**Website:**

Username:       Email:

Password:

Security Question 1:

Security Answer 1:

Security Question 2:

Security Answer 2:

Notes:

**Website:**

Username:      Email:

Password:

Security Question 1:

Security Answer 1:

Security Question 2:

Security Answer 2:

Notes:

**Website:**

Username:      Email:

Password:

Security Question 1:

Security Answer 1:

Security Question 2:

Security Answer 2:

Notes:

**Website:**

Username:      Email:

Password:

Security Question 1:

Security Answer 1:

Security Question 2:

Security Answer 2:

Notes:

## Website:

Username:                          Email:

Password:

Security Question 1:

Security Answer 1:

Security Question 2:

Security Answer 2:

Notes:

## Website:

Username:                          Email:

Password:

Security Question 1:

Security Answer 1:

Security Question 2:

Security Answer 2:

Notes:

## Website:

Username:                          Email:

Password:

Security Question 1:

Security Answer 1:

Security Question 2:

Security Answer 2:

Notes:

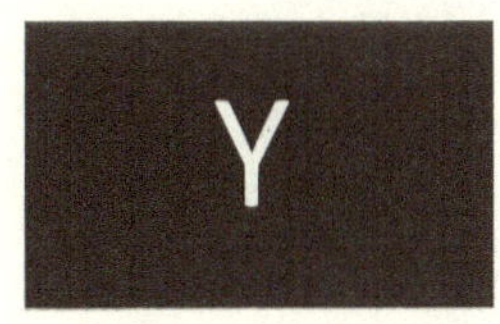



Website:

Username:                                          Email:

Password:

Security Question 1:

Security Answer 1:

Security Question 2:

Security Answer 2:

Notes:


Website:

Username:                                          Email:

Password:

Security Question 1:

Security Answer 1:

Security Question 2:

Security Answer 2:

Notes:


Website:

Username:                                          Email:

Password:

Security Question 1:

Security Answer 1:

Security Question 2:

Security Answer 2:

Notes:

Website:

Username: Email:

Password:

Security Question 1:

Security Answer 1:

Security Question 2:

Security Answer 2:

Notes:

Website:

Username: Email:

Password:

Security Question 1:

Security Answer 1:

Security Question 2:

Security Answer 2:

Notes:

Website:

Username: Email:

Password:

Security Question 1:

Security Answer 1:

Security Question 2:

Security Answer 2:

Notes:

## Website:

Username:                       Email:

Password:

Security Question 1:

Security Answer 1:

Security Question 2:

Security Answer 2:

Notes:

## Website:

Username:                       Email:

Password:

Security Question 1:

Security Answer 1:

Security Question 2:

Security Answer 2:

Notes:

## Website:

Username:                       Email:

Password:

Security Question 1:

Security Answer 1:

Security Question 2:

Security Answer 2:

Notes:

Website:

Username:                                    Email:

Password:

Security Question 1:

Security Answer 1:

Security Question 2:

Security Answer 2:

Notes:


Website:

Username:                                    Email:

Password:

Security Question 1:

Security Answer 1:

Security Question 2:

Security Answer 2:

Notes:


Website:

Username:                                    Email:

Password:

Security Question 1:

Security Answer 1:

Security Question 2:

Security Answer 2:

Notes:

## Website:

| | |
|---|---|
| Username: | Email: |

Password:

Security Question 1:

Security Answer 1:

Security Question 2:

Security Answer 2:

Notes:

## Website:

| | |
|---|---|
| Username: | Email: |

Password:

Security Question 1:

Security Answer 1:

Security Question 2:

Security Answer 2:

Notes:

## Website:

| | |
|---|---|
| Username: | Email: |

Password:

Security Question 1:

Security Answer 1:

Security Question 2:

Security Answer 2:

Notes:

# Z

Website:

Username:                                    Email:

Password:

Security Question 1:

Security Answer 1:

Security Question 2:

Security Answer 2:

Notes:

Website:

Username:                                    Email:

Password:

Security Question 1:

Security Answer 1:

Security Question 2:

Security Answer 2:

Notes:

Website:

Username:                                    Email:

Password:

Security Question 1:

Security Answer 1:

Security Question 2:

Security Answer 2:

Notes:

**Z**

**Website:**

Username:      Email:

Password:

Security Question 1:

Security Answer 1:

Security Question 2:

Security Answer 2:

Notes:

**Website:**

Username:      Email:

Password:

Security Question 1:

Security Answer 1:

Security Question 2:

Security Answer 2:

Notes:

**Website:**

Username:      Email:

Password:

Security Question 1:

Security Answer 1:

Security Question 2:

Security Answer 2:

Notes:

# Z

Website:

Username:     Email:

Password:

Security Question 1:

Security Answer 1:

Security Question 2:

Security Answer 2:

Notes:

Website:

Username:     Email:

Password:

Security Question 1:

Security Answer 1:

Security Question 2:

Security Answer 2:

Notes:

Website:

Username:     Email:

Password:

Security Question 1:

Security Answer 1:

Security Question 2:

Security Answer 2:

Notes:

Z

Website:

Username:                    Email:

Password:

Security Question 1:

Security Answer 1:

Security Question 2:

Security Answer 2:

Notes:

Website:

Username:                    Email:

Password:

Security Question 1:

Security Answer 1:

Security Question 2:

Security Answer 2:

Notes:

Website:

Username:                    Email:

Password:

Security Question 1:

Security Answer 1:

Security Question 2:

Security Answer 2:

Notes:

Z

**Website:**

Username: ___________________  Email: ___________________

Password: ___________________

Security Question 1: ___________________

Security Answer 1: ___________________

Security Question 2: ___________________

Security Answer 2: ___________________

Notes: ___________________

**Website:**

Username: ___________________  Email: ___________________

Password: ___________________

Security Question 1: ___________________

Security Answer 1: ___________________

Security Question 2: ___________________

Security Answer 2: ___________________

Notes: ___________________

**Website:**

Username: ___________________  Email: ___________________

Password: ___________________

Security Question 1: ___________________

Security Answer 1: ___________________

Security Question 2: ___________________

Security Answer 2: ___________________

Notes: ___________________

**Website:**

Username:                    Email:

Password:

Security Question 1:

Security Answer 1:

Security Question 2:

Security Answer 2:

Notes:

**Website:**

Username:                    Email:

Password:

Security Question 1:

Security Answer 1:

Security Question 2:

Security Answer 2:

Notes:

**Website:**

Username:                    Email:

Password:

Security Question 1:

Security Answer 1:

Security Question 2:

Security Answer 2:

Notes: